G000025549

Kathy Lette's

GIRL talk

IN THE PINK

Kathy Lette In the Pink
Published by Kinkajou
Copyright © Kathy Lette 2015

Kathy Lette has asserted her right under the Copyright,
Designs & Patents Act 1988 to be identified as the author
of this work.

Illustrations copyright © Frances Lincoln Limited 2015

A catalogue record for this book is available from the
British Library.

Illustrations by Mark Mason.
Design by www.smartdesignstudio.co.uk

Kinkajou is an imprint of Frances Lincoln Limited
74-77 White Lion Street, London N1 9PF, United Kingdom.

ISBN: 978-0-7112-3720-9

Printed in China

9 8 7 6 5 4 3 2 1

Kathy Lette's GIRL talk

IN THE PINK

kinkajou

Girl Talk

It's still a man's world. Women don't have equal pay – we're getting 75 pence in the pound. We're also getting concussion hitting our heads on the glass ceiling, and we're expected to clean it whilst up there. Clearly, any woman who calls herself a 'post feminist' has kept her wonder bra and burnt her brains.

But we women do have one powerful weapon in our armoury – **Girl Talk**. Yes, men are physically stronger, but women are more verbally dexterous. Apparently we use an average of 400 extra words in our daily vocabulary. If a woman can shoot from the lip with a well-aimed one liner, she can give a man quip-lash which will either charm, disarm or harm him (if he turns out to keep fit by doing step aerobics off his own ego).

Women are each other's human wonder bras – uplifting, supportive and making each other look bigger and better. The wit and wisdom of this book will not only offer some pun-in-cheek female solidarity but will also help readers hone their black belts in tongue-fu."

Kathy Lette ♡

CHAPTER ONE

DATING

I'M NAMED AFTER A DIARY, SO CLEARLY, I'VE HAD MANY DATES. DATING MEANS GAMBLING WITH FATE AND LOSING SO MANY TIMES, A GIRL GETS ROULETTE-RASH. (MEN PROBLEMS: NOW *THERE'S* A TAUTOLOGY!) SO, AFTER MANY YEARS AS AN AMOROUS ANTHROPOLOGIST, HERE ARE MY TOP TIPS FOR MATING AND DATING.

- What are women looking for?

OH, NOTHING SPECIAL. AS LONG AS HE HAS PECTORALS, A PhD, A NICE BUM, A NON-SEXIST ATTITUDE, A TOP TAN, A WELL-READ PENIS, CAN COOK SOUFFLÈS, ARM-WRESTLE CROCODILES, WANTS A LOVING RELATIONSHIP AND CAN PROVIDE BONE-MARROW-MELTING SEX...

Now, is that too much to ask of a billionaire?

DON'T WAIT TO BE RESCUED BY A
Knight in Shining Armani.

A GIRL SHOULD STAND ON HER OWN TWO
stilettos.

AVOID MEN WHO ARE
FLUENT IN BODY
LANGUAGE.
YES, HE HAS THE

gift of the grab.

BUT WHEN HE
ASKS YOU FOR A
"COFFEE", IT'LL BE IN
PERVERTED COMMAS.

NEVER *DELUDE*
YOURSELF THAT YOU
CAN

change a man...

THE ONLY TIME YOU
CAN DO THAT IS
OUT OF A NAPPY
WHEN HE'S A BABY!

AVOID MEN
WHO DRIVE A

meno-porsche.

HIS NUMBER PLATE
SHOULD READ
"MIDLIFE CRISIS".

WANTED:

Toy Boy –

MUST ADORE ME,
NOT BORE ME
AND DO ALL
MY CHORES
FOR ME.

DATE AN
HISTORIAN –
HE'LL NEVER
THINK YOU'RE
too old.

CHAPTER TWO

MARRIAGE

IT'S SO BLISSFUL TO DISCOVER YOUR ALTAR-EGO. BUT WHAT ARE THE BEST WAYS TO AVOID THE MOURNING AFTER THE KNOT BEFORE? HERE ARE MY TOP TIPS...

IF YOUR BOYFRIEND PROPOSES WITH –

"Let's just do it, for better or worse..."

CLARIFY EXACTLY HOW MUCH WORSE?

IS HE GOING TO START FLOSSING

OR FARTING IN BED?...

ANY WOMAN WHO SAYS SHE GETS *high on housework* HAS OBVIOUSLY INHALED **WAY** TOO MUCH CLEANING FLUID.

MANY COUPLES
BREAK UP
FOR RELIGIOUS
REASONS -
HE THINKS HE'S
A *God*
AND WELL, SHE
JUST DOESN'T.

IT IS SCIENTIFICALLY PROVEN THAT NO WOMAN EVER SHOT HER HUSBAND WHILE HE WAS VACUUMING.

WHAT DOES A
MARRIED WOMAN
WANT IN BED?

Breakfast.

MAKE SURE
YOUR HUBBY
UNDERSTANDS THAT
THE *Kama Sutra* IS
NOT AN INDIAN
TAKEAWAY AND A
'MUTUAL ORGASM' IS
NOT AN INSURANCE
COMPANY.

CHAPTER THREE

PREGNANCY

PREGNANCY IS THE TIME IN A WOMAN'S LIFE WHEN SHE DISCOVERS THAT THERE IS ACTUALLY SOMETHING WORSE THAN GETTING HER PERIOD. *NOT GETTING IT*. A PREGNANCY TEST IS THE ONE TEST YOU CAN'T CHEAT ON. WHAT DO YOU CALL A WOMAN WHO USES THE RHYTHM METHOD?... *MUM!*

OVER HALF OF ALL MARRIAGES END IN DIVORCE, SO BEFORE HAVING UNPROTECTED SEX, ASK YOURSELF – IS THIS THE MAN WHOSE NAME YOU WANT TO SEE ON THE CHILD MAINTENANCE CHEQUES EVERY MONTH?

WHAT'S THE
DIFFERENCE BETWEEN
A PREGNANT WOMAN
AND A LIGHT BULB?

*You can unscrew
a light bulb.*

MANY FATHERS *chicken out* OF THEIR OBLIGATION TO THEIR EGGS.

A PATERNITY SUIT IS **NOT** THE *latest look* IN MEN'S LEISUREWEAR.

CHAPTER FOUR

CHILDBIRTH

NATURAL CHILDBIRTH IS A CASE OF KEEPING A STIFF UPPER LABIA... WE'VE DONE DRUGS ALL OUR LIVES. WHY STOP NOW?! OH, AND IF THE FATHER OF YOUR CHILD DOESN'T TURN UP TO THE LABOUR WARD, DON'T CONTRACT PRE-NATAL DEPRESSION. JUST UNSETTLE HIM BY EXPLAINING THAT THE ONLY GOOD THING ABOUT BEING A WOMAN IS NEVER HAVING TO WORRY ABOUT WHO THE MOTHER IS.

IT'S STONE AGE WHAT HAPPENS TO YOU IN LABOUR. IT'S COMPLETELY PREHISTORIC. LYING ON THAT BIRTHING TABLE, ADOPTION STARTS TO LOOK LIKE A VERY ATTRACTIVE ALTERNATIVE. IF YOU EVER HAD ANY DOUBT ABOUT THE GENDER OF GOD, YOU NOW **KNOW** HE'S A BLOKE.

IF YOUR HUSBAND
DOESN'T WANT TO BE
THERE AT THE BIRTH,
TELL HIM THAT, HEY,
YOU DON'T WANT TO
BE THERE!
If he was there when it went in, HE SHOULD
BE THERE WHEN IT
COMES OUT!

If a man were asked to grow an alien in his belly for forty weeks, causing *varicose veins, wind, amnesia and halitosis,* followed by thirty-seven hours of intense agony – even James Bond would decline on the grounds that it was **TOO DAMN DANGEROUS.**

MOTHER NATURE
IS A BAD MIDWIFE.
FORGET BEANBAGS
AND WATER BIRTHS.
JUST OPT FOR THE
"Full-Anaesthetic-Elective-
Caesarean-Wake-Me-
When-It's-Over-And-The-
Make-Up-Artist's-Here"
APPROACH.

DON'T FILM THE BIRTH.
SO MUCH MORE
FUN TO FILM THE
conception.

CHAPTER FIVE

MOTHERHOOD

THE FIRST 40 YEARS OF MOTHERHOOD ARE ALWAYS THE HARDEST. IT HELPS TO REMEMBER THAT YOU HAVE A SECRET WEAPON – THE HOME VIDEOS OF YOUR KIDS' BIRTHS, ENABLING YOU TO REPLAY THE EMBARRASSING AGONY TO YOUR CHILDREN'S FRIENDS ON SIGNIFICANT BIRTHDAYS. FOR OTHER MOTHERING SURVIVAL TIPS, READ ON.

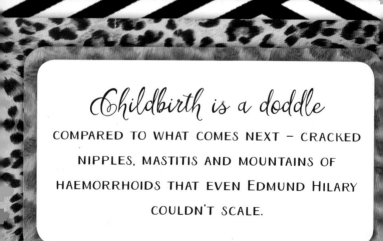

Childbirth is a doddle

COMPARED TO WHAT COMES NEXT – CRACKED NIPPLES, MASTITIS AND MOUNTAINS OF HAEMORRHOIDS THAT EVEN EDMUND HILARY COULDN'T SCALE.

As a breast feeder you are now a

24 HOUR CATERING SERVICE -

you are

Meals on Heels.

THE ONLY RESPONSE
TO A BABY MONITOR
IS TO TALK INTO IT
AND SAY,

"I'M SORRY, BUT THE
WORKING MOTHER YOU
ARE TRYING TO REACH
IS TEMPORARILY
DISCONNECTED. PLEASE
TRY AGAIN LATER."

KIDS ARE LIKE

Ikea appliances –

YOU HAVE NO IDEA
HOW MUCH ASSEMBLY
IS REQUIRED UNTIL
IT'S *WAY TOO LATE!*

YOU'LL KNOW YOU'RE DEFINITELY *A few nappies short of a packet* OF PAMPERS WHEN YOU FIND YOURSELF SITTING IN THE PLAYPEN WITH THE BABY SITTING OUT OF IT, GIVING YOU ONE OF THOSE DISAPPOINTED '*HEY, I GAVE YOU THE BEST YEAR OF MY LIFE!*' LOOKS.

WORKING MUMS JUGGLE
SO MUCH WE COULD
BE IN THE CIRQUE
DU SOLEIL. JUST
REMEMBER THAT
you can have it all,
ONLY NOT ALL
AT ONCE.

DON'T EVER LET YOUR
KIDS ADDRESS YOU BY
YOUR FIRST NAME.
THIS IS NOT ONLY
nauseatingly trendy, BUT
WAY TOO INFORMAL.
I MEAN, IT'S NOT AS IF
YOU'VE KNOWN EACH
OTHER VERY LONG.

A BALANCED MEAL IS WHATEVER STAYS ON THE SPOON EN ROUTE TO A BABY'S MOUTH.

"Controlled crying" IS THE ART OF NOT SHATTERING INTO TEARS WHEN YOUR TODDLER ACCIDENTLY WIPES MARMITE ALL OVER YOUR NEW *designer dress.*

CHAPTER SIX

WOMEN ARE THE BUTT OF GOD'S BIOLOGICAL JOKE. JUST THINK OF ALL THE THINGS WE GO THROUGH, FROM PERIODS TO PREGNANCY TO MASTITIS TO MENOPAUSE AND THEN, JUST WHEN EVERYTHING GOES QUIET, DO YOU KNOW WHAT HAPPENS? *YOU GROW A BEARD.* IS THAT FAIR I ASK YOU? BUT DON'T RESORT TO COSMETIC SURGERY TO STAY YOUNG. I MEAN HAVE YOU BEEN TO L.A.? IT'S A WRINKLE-FREE ZONE. THERE IS NO LAW OF GRAVITY. SKIN SAGS UPWARDS. BASICALLY, THEY JUST DRAG EVERYTHING UP. YOUR ANKLES BECOME KNEES. YOUR KNEES YOUR NAVEL. YOUR CLITORIS BECOMES YOUR CHIN…. THAT'S HOW YOU SPOT A RECIPIENT OF COSMETIC SURGERY. YOU LOOK FOR A WOMAN WHO IS RUBBING THAT PARTICULAR PART OF HER ANATOMY A LITTLE TOO VIGOROUSLY. ACTUALLY THE BEST WAYS TO STAY YOUNG ARE LAUGHING AND ORGASMS …OH, AND A DIMMER SWITCH – GREATEST BEAUTY AID KNOWN TO WOMAN KIND!

FORGET FACELIFTS.

MEN SHOULD LEARN TO

read between our lines.

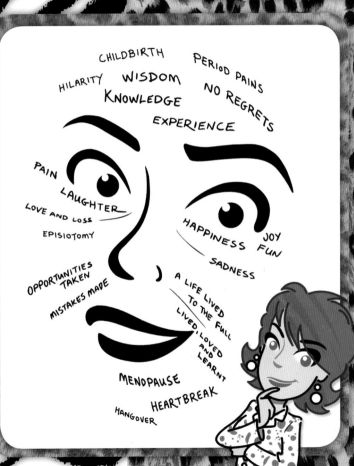

OUR MUMS ALWAYS TOLD US THAT *beauty comes from within.* YEAH. WITH A JAR MARKED

Estee Lauder.

IF YOUR TEENAGE DAUGHTER HITS YOU AND KICKS YOU AND SAYS "*I WISH YOU'D JUST DIE!*" TAKE A BIG SWIG OF *wine*, DRAW BACK ON A *cigarette* AND REPLY, "*I'M DOING MY BEST DARLING.*"

The bottom line is –
the lobotomised line is –
WHY WOULD YOU WANT
A MAN WHO **ONLY** WANTS
YOU BECAUSE YOU'RE SILICONE
FROM TITS TO TOE?
AND YOU WOULDN'T
REALLY, WOULD
YOU?

Cowboy cosmetic surgeons
ARE **NOT** REAL
DOCTORS. THE
REASON THEY WEAR
THOSE LITTLE GREEN
MASKS IS SO THEY
CAN'T BE RECOGNISED
IF ANYTHING
GOES WRONG.

Congrats!

You now have a Black Belt in **Tongue Fu!**

The reason why men like intelligent women?
Because opposites attract!

Always remember that **witty** lasts longer than **pretty.**

Now go forth and be fabulous!

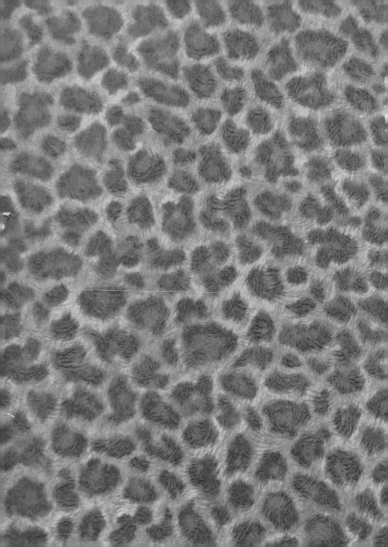